THE
MARRIAGE
PLAYBOOK

Rev. George Lasley III
Stephanie Lasley

TRILOGY CHRISTIAN PUBLISHERS
Tustin, CA

Trilogy Christian Publishers

A Wholly Owned Subsidiary of Trinity Broadcasting Network

2442 Michelle Drive

Tustin, CA 92780

For information, address Trilogy Christian Publishing

Rights Department, 2442 Michelle Drive, Tustin, Ca 92780.

Trilogy Christian Publishing/ TBN and colophon are trademarks of Trinity Broadcasting Network.

For information about special discounts for bulk purchases, please contact Trilogy Christian Publishing.

Manufactured in the United States of America

Cover image: Photo by Andrew Neel from Pexels

10 9 8 7 6 5 4 3 2 1

Library of Congress Cataloging-in-Publication Data is available.

ISBN 978-1-64088-648-3

ISBN 978-1-64088-649-0 (e-book)

Contents

Author George Lasley

Team Ownership: God

Coach: Husband

Star Player: Wife

Author George Lasley

1. God

2. Husband

3. Wife

4. Child

5. Spiritual Advisors

Role Players

Kids

Drafts and Incorporating Subsitutions

Blended Families and Childbirth

No Trade Acquisition Allowed!

Dedication

This book is dedicated to:

The Potts, Schofields, Whites, Conleys, Prices, Davises, Lewises, Lasters, and Lasleys. We are tremendously thankful for our host of friends for your thoughts and prayers. Your love and support have encouraged us beyond measures.

Foreword

The book's purpose provides boundaries for a marriage. God's Word is unlike any literature and it cannot be duplicated. It is a divine revelation of what God wants for humanity as opposed to what humanity wants for itself.

The authors attend to provide biblical clarity, and applicable and practical analyses, drawing the reader to learn valuable aspects about the institution of marriage according to Scripture. Marriage displays the love of Christ and there are several biblical insinuations. Ephesians 5:32 states, "This is a great mystery: but I speak concerning Christ and the church." God is expressing the importance of His love for the world.

The authors encourage marriage and the process of never giving up, for marriage between a man and woman is different than any relationship. A relationship may fail because of indifference; whereas a marriage, *if properly instituted by God, lasts forever.*

REV. GEORGE LASLEY III & STEPHANIE LASLEY

Preface

The focal point of the book will prove analogies that provide countless scenarios that address many of the complex issues in marriage. The authors use imagery to help the reader visualize the intent and purpose of the book that serve as a guide for anyone who aspires to be married or remained married. The spiritual and practical advice offer information that helps conceptualize God's point of view. Each chapter was chosen carefully, constructed to convey a precise message.

REV. GEORGE LASLEY III & STEPHANIE LASLEY

Acknowledgements

Nothing is possible without our Lord and Savior Jesus the Christ. His unwavering love has withstood the test of time, providing a vision and the provision to write our first book together. This testament alone illustrates the love of Christ and the compassion He shows His people. Two college students walking the halls at the University of Wisconsin Parkside cannot imagine the blessings that have been received. God has blessed us so much that we are compelled to help others in the same way the Lord has provided.

Finally, it is only suitable to acknowledge our spiritual leaders and the administration, faculty, staff, and students at Milwaukee Lutheran High School. Their willingness to help and support made it possible to write *The Marriage Playbook*.

Introduction

The creation of marriage is beautiful. For a marriage to remain beautiful, the creator needs to be interwoven in the fabric.

God grant us patience, teamwork, and commitment. Protect us individually and collectively from seen and unseen dangers. In Jesus' name we pray, amen.

REV. GEORGE LASLEY III & STEPHANIE LASLEY

Prologue

The Marriage Playbook

"And He answered and said to them, Have you not read that He who made them at the beginning made them male and female, and said, For this reason a man shall leave his father and mother and be joined to his wife, and the two shall become one flesh? So then, they are no longer two but one flesh.
Therefore, what God has joined together, let not man separate."
Matthew 19:4-6 (NKJV)

Rev. George Lasley III, BA, M.Div.
Stephanie Lasley, BBA

The Team Structure

The Best Fit For Team Chemistry

"Then the rib which the Lord had taken from man He made into a woman, and He brought her to the man" (Genesis: 2:22).

A marriage needs to be constructed like any team. Any team needs a structure that fits the need of everyone involved.

God (The Father, Son, and Holy Spirit) is the team's president, CEO, and general manager. The purpose of ownership is to fulfill a vision and provide the resources needed to succeed.

Unlike basketball, God does not need to put in a bid for ownership. However, the organizational structure needs to buy into the owner's vision. If a complete buy-in is not made, the infrastructure of the team is threatened. Coaches are usually fired, and teams underachieve.

To ensure success, any marriage needs to have frequent team meetings with the owner in prayer. This purpose is to bring the team together to hear what the owner wants. Each team is unique, so all teams are structured for different reasons, but for one ultimate purpose. The end goal for any team (the institution of marriage) is the same, *The Finals.* Unlike basketball, competing with others is not an essential component; practicing on past mistakes are.

Notes:

_____

_____

_____

_____

_____

_____

_____

_____

_____

_____

_____

Phase 1
Discussion Questions, Thoughts, & Topics
The Team Structure

It is important to address the significance.

1. How would you identify your religious affiliation and spiritual identity?

   _____

   _____

   _____

2. To ensure that your spouse has the same spiritual identity, discuss it together.

   _____

   _____

   _____

   If there are other relative aspects, converse about the issues.

3. What challenges do you foresee regarding Phase 1?

   _____

   _____

   _____

It is suggested to answer the Discussion Questions before proceeding to Phase 2.

"For the husband is the head of the wife as Christ is the head of the church, his body, of which he is the Savior" (Ephesians 5:23).

The Husband's Role

Becoming or Remaining Spiritually Driven

The statement "Be a man" is ambiguous. A husband needs to know his role within a marriage to be effective. "Be a man" is a secular term that promotes outward strength rather than inner growth. Vulnerability is significant. The husband plays the role of a coach. He needs to be spiritually driven to convey the plays "scriptures" to his family "team". Without solidifying this essential role, the team structure is lost.

There are great teams that play poorly due to the team's inability to foster an environment that allows the coach to facilitate team chemistry. The husband must also be willing to listen to the voice of the Lord to sustain him as they both draft plays. A marriage is constantly evolving, because no one stays the same, including the star player (the wife) and the role players (the children). Any good coach is not set in his ways; if he is, he prevents the team from evolving in critical areas. The coach must recognize potential weaknesses and structure a plan to ensure sustainability through difficult and unexpected situations.

The Husband's Prayer

Lord help_____ (The Husband's Name) to be obedient to God, his family, and himself. Protect his mind, body, and spirit. Help him guide his family spiritually, mentally, and financially. In Jesus' name we pray, amen.

Notes:

_____

_____

_____

_____

_____

_____

_____

_____

_____

_____

_____

_____

_____

_____

_____

_____

_____

"Who can find a virtuous wife? For her worth is far above rubies" (Proverbs 31:10).

The Wife's Role
Dynamic Execution

The wife has a critical role to play in ensuring that the plays drafted are executed. A team's success depends on the star player's commitment to trust the ownership and coach. Throughout history, many great players have had many excellent individual statistics but were unable to reach the finals because of their selfishness. If the coach and the star player lack team chemistry, who do not adhere to the structural elements of their team, finger pointing usually occurs and failures follow.

However, the all-time greats can make those around them better; this includes the coaching staff. The star player produces highlights and can manage the team on the floor. **Her execution is dynamic** because the wife must help the coach provide for the role players, which in this analogy are children. Star players need to be trusted, because responsibility is thrusted upon them.

The Wife's Prayer

Lord enable _____ (The Wife's Name) to be virtuous in all of her affairs, to guard her heart against distractions, and lead her family and build up her husband and children. It is in Jesus' name we pray, amen.

Notes:

_____

_____

_____

_____

_____

_____

_____

_____

_____

_____

_____

_____

_____

_____

_____

_____

_____

REV. GEORGE LASLEY III & STEPHANIE LASLEY

The Starting Five

No Trade Acquisitions Allowed!

*"From whom the whole body, joined and knit
together by what every joint supplies, according to
the effective working by which every part
does its share, causes growth of the body for
the edifying of itself in love"
(Ephesians 4:16).*

The starting five must be cohesive. One may ask themselves, "Who are a part of the starting five, since I was instructed not to let outside sources ruin my marriage?" If a basketball team only has two players in the starting lineup, the team will lose every game.

As in "Phase 1", God, the husband, and the wife are the most essential. However, there were two unaddressed aspects. Children and a spiritual advisor are essential role players. In many marriages, the couple does not think of the fourth and fifth player; these two players can cause the team to lose, thinking that their role is insignificant.

All marriages should have a no-trade acquisition clause. Many marriages suffer from the inability to blend families. People who get married after having children often neglect their potential, misplacing time and energy.

In certain contract clauses, there is a no-trade acquisition. Not only should this clause apply for marriages, but this aspect should be a frame of mind. There are no trade deadlines in marriages. It is the responsibility of the coach "husband" and the star player "wife," who is also the coach on the floor to speak with the owner "God" about how and when to blend their families.

The other component of the starting five is a spiritual advisor. Advisors are needed to help with teamwork to ensure that the foundation aligns with God's Holy Word. Choosing the right spiritual advisor is key to winning.

Phase 2 Prayer

Lord strengthen the _____ (The Family's Name). Help the children become more spiritual in all they do. Help our family blend together. We rebuke any demonic spirits in our household and any generational curse that may exist. It is in Jesus' name we pray, amen.

Notes:

_____

_____

_____

_____

_____

_____

_____

_____

_____

_____

_____

_____

_____

_____

_____

_____

_____

_____

_____

_____

_____

_____

_____

_____

Phase 2

Discussion Questions, Thoughts, & Topics

The Starting Five

Marital Roles are essential to any marriage.

1. What are your marital roles?

    _____

    _____

    _____

    _____

    _____

    _____

    _____

2. Will your team succeed the way it is currently constructed?

    _____

    _____

    _____

    _____

    _____

    _____

    _____

It is suggested to answer the Discussion Questions before proceeding to Phase 3.

The Second Team

An Important Responsibility

"You are the salt of the earth. But if the salt loses its saltiness, how can it be made salty again? It is no longer good for anything, except to be thrown out and trampled underfoot. You are the light of the world. A town built on a hill cannot be hidden"
(Matthew 5:13-14).

In Phases 1 and 2, the team structure was presented, which includes the big three: God, the husband, and the wife. In this phase, the second team's responsibility is introduced. Like any basketball team, the rest of the team plays an essential role. The second team consists of younger children and in-laws. Children should be raised with Godly discipline, exemplifying God's love. As indirectly noted, children may have a dual role. Depending on age and maturity, the role can be enlarged. Whatever lacks in a marriage will affect the parent's and child's relationship. Like a basketball team, the starters set the precedent of a team's behavior.

A good team will show a commitment, positive temperament, enthusiasm, and eagerness to work together to win. **Children will behave how they see their parents behave.** The same holds true for in-laws. It is the spouse's responsibility to cultivate the relationship between his or her parents and spouse. For example, a wife should show respect and honor towards her husband in her parents' presence and in return, the parents will exemplify the same behavior. The same holds true for the husband. It becomes the responsibility of the husband to lay the foundation for the in-law/spouse relationship. This is not an easy task if your parents need to adjust to your marriage.

The more the expectations are set, the more the parents will become accustomed to the boundaries in their relationship with your spouse. It is imperative to know, this only applies to healthy relationships. In Matthew 5:13-14, it speaks about the importance of remaining faithful and respectful to God and our spouse in front of others. This certain discipline will ultimately lead to peace in your interactions with in-laws. Just as we ought to become trained and disciplined by God's Word, we should use that same willingness to show the same respect to our spouses.

Phase 3 Prayer

Father help me to show my husband/wife respect so that it will show others how to treat my spouse. Thank you for the peace you have given our family. In Jesus' name, amen.

Notes:

_____

_____

_____

_____

_____

_____

_____

_____

_____

_____

_____

_____

_____

_____

_____

_____

_____

Phase 3
Discussion Questions, Thoughts, & Topics
The Second Team

Important Marital Decisions

1. Are there any viewpoints regarding your inclusion or the creation of a second team?

_____

_____

_____

_____

2. How will your second team be established, cultivated, supported, and executed?

_____

_____

_____

_____

3. Create a list of your second team, including an attached or added timeline.

_____

_____

_____

_____

_____

_____

4. Who will ensure the timeline of your future plans are met?

_____

_____

_____

_____

_____

_____

_____

5. Will responsibilities be divided or completed together?

_____

_____

_____

_____

_____

_____

_____

_____

_____

It is suggested to answer the Discussion Questions before proceeding to Phase 4.

Communication

Be Slow to Speak

"So then, my beloved brethren, let every man be swift to hear, slow to speak, slow to wrath"
(James 1:19).

Have you ever had a conversation with someone and had to repeat yourself several times because that person was not listening to anything you were saying? Communication is the ability to talk AND listen. Most of us get the talking part just fine, but it is the listening that gets us in trouble. One way to communicate with God is through prayer. Prayer is a clear and direct avenue to God, and it is also a way for God to communicate back to you. Some may think that prayer is just a time to give God a list of our wants and needs. We must humble ourselves and be willing to receive God's Word.

Communicating in a marriage is key. A wife must be able to speak her truths, wants, and needs and be willing to listen to the truths, wants, and needs of her husband.

During a basketball game, we will see players communicate with each other. If a player misses a shot, sometimes you can catch a glimpse of a teammate giving constructive criticism. In the same fashion, if a player makes a shot, he or she is cheered on by teammates. This holds true for a marriage. If your teammate (spouse) needs a reminder of the things you need and want, we must be able to humbly communicate. How can we possibly be satisfied if we do not speak of the things that we need (James 4:2-3)? On the other hand, positive affirmations are a powerful way to create and improve a positive environment in your home.

Phase 4 Prayer

God thank you for your wisdom, and aid us to become better communicators. Help us to be better listeners as we pray and enable us the ability to listen to our spouse's verbal and nonverbal communication. In Jesus' name, amen.

Notes:

_____

_____

_____

_____

_____

_____

_____

_____

_____

_____

_____

_____

_____

_____

_____

_____

_____

_____

_____

_____

_____

_____

Phase 4
Discussion Questions, Thoughts, & Topics
Communication

Communication is fundamentally important.

1. How do you currently communicate? *Keep in mind, communication involves speaking and listening.*

_____

_____

_____

_____

_____

_____

_____

2. How well do you currently communicate and how can you improve?

_____

_____

_____

_____

_____

_____

_____

3. Discuss potential ways to prevent disagreements and how disputes will be confronted?

_____

_____

_____

_____

_____

_____

4. How do you prefer to handle disputes?

_____

_____

_____

_____

_____

_____

It is suggested to answer the Discussion Questions before proceeding to Phase 5.

REV. GEORGE LASLEY III & STEPHANIE LASLEY

Team Meetings

The Game Plan, Roles, and Expectations

"For as we have many members in one body, but all the members do not have the same function" (Romans 12:4).

Couples often have a busy routine with kids, work, family, and other obligations with little to no flexibility in their schedules, which means little to no time for each other or God. Many marriages suffer because of a disconnection. We believe that when two people are 100 percent committed to living the Word of God, they create a strong foundation. Think of commitment as a battery percentage on your device. When your device is at one hundred percent, it performs quicker and lights up brighter. Once the battery starts losing its power, it gets weaker and ultimately shuts off. The same will happen in our individual lives. It is essential to take time to recharge and reconnect with one another. We can get so caught-up in our routine that we neglect to make time for spouses and reflect on the things we have not accomplished, so re-position your plans and goals.

When we lose connection with God, it is like losing a battery adapter. When our battery runs low, God is the One who can recharge us. Personal routines can distract the team's ability to function. God did not join a man and a woman together for them to isolate oneself. Marriage is an ever-lasting commitment between two people joined together as one (Mark 10:8) to serve God. Mark 10:9 states, "therefore what God has joined together, let not man separate."

It does not mean that the enemy won't try to stop God's plan for your marriage. However, nothing should come between a marriage and to make sure of this, spouses should meet regularly to establish their game plan. The game plan protects and covers the covenant that God has established.

Just like during time-outs or at halftime in a basketball game, players meet with their coaches to determine a play; the plan to defeat the opposing team. In a marriage, this is done through prayer. Team meetings will also help spouses communicate their roles and be held accountable for any mishaps. Each should communicate his or her expectations to ensure that the goals set forth is being accomplished. Miscommunication is often the cause of arguements, so meet with your spouse regularly to deter mishaps, frustrations, and letdowns.

Phase 5 Prayer

Holy Father allow us to stay connected. Please give us the strength to pray for any attacks that may come against our marriage. Give us a clear direction and allow us to be comfortable with communicating our expectations to each other. We thank you for the ability to serve you and welcome your Holy Spirit into our lives and our marriage. We pray that all marriages would be a blessing. In Jesus' name, amen.

Notes:

_____

_____

_____

_____

_____

_____

_____

_____

_____

_____

_____

_____

Phase 5
Discussion Questions, Thoughts, & Topics
Team Meetings

1. When will your team meetings be held? Discuss the location, time, and date.

   _____

   _____

   _____

   _____

2. Think of the things to discuss and how to address issues effectively.

   _____

   _____

   _____

   _____

   _____

3. Have fun and be encouraging.

   _____

   _____

   _____

   _____

It is suggested to answer the Discussion Questions before proceeding to Phase 6.

REV. GEORGE LASLEY III & STEPHANIE LASLEY

Studying the Plays

Study to Show Thyself Approved

"This Book of the Law shall not depart from your mouth, but you shall meditate in it day and night, that you may observe to do according to all that is written in it. For then you will make your way prosperous, and then you will have good success"
(Joshua 1:8).

Studying plays is essential when it comes to team chemistry and team dominance. One must study the Bible, their spouse, and their team chemistry to ensure that everything is intact. There have been many talented teams who tried to rely heavily on their gifts and talents, which are needed, but without trusting in the coaches' strategies, the team loses focus. The players should know their roles and responsibilities on and off the court. Many coaches require their team to learn the team's offensive and defensive strategies in the off-season. Sometimes plays are instituted throughout the season, and each person needs to make time to get familiar with their playbook. It is apparent which players have seriously studied, conversed, and adapted to the plays and team strategy.

For married couples, the Bible is the playbook. It explains martial, parental, and personal responsibilities. Joshua explains that the book of the laws should not depart from one's mouth. If only one person is adhering to the spiritual direction of God, this is a cause for concern. There is no better way to learn about what God expects for each person than from the Bible.

As noted earlier, team chemistry is paramount. Chemistry comes from living according to the Word of God. 2 Timothy 2:15 speaks about being hearers and doers of the Word. This concept is just as important in marriages. One cannot decide what scripture to obey and what scripture to ignore because of personal conveniences. My wife often talks about how we have changed throughout our marriage.

Scripture offers martial advice about how to adjust to our spouses and oneself. If one needs help with what plays "scriptures" to study, refer to the scriptures at the beginning of each phase.

Phase 6 Prayer

Lord, please encourage _____ (Husband's Name) and _____ (Wife's Name) to study the Word of God *more* to show thyself approved so we can recite the appropriate scriptures in the time of need. In Jesus' name, amen.

Notes:

_____

_____

_____

_____

_____

_____

_____

_____

_____

_____

_____

_____

_____

_____

_____

_____

_____

Phase 6
Discussion Questions, Thoughts, & Topics
Studying the Plays

Studying Scripture will impact you and your marriage. *God speaks through Scripture, expressing the importance of dedicating time to read scripture independently and collectively.*

1. How much time do you dedicate to reading Scripture?

_____

_____

_____

_____

_____

_____

_____

2. How important are biblical messages to you?

- -

- -

- -

- -

- -

- -

3. Are you willing to take the necessary time to read and study?

_____

_____

_____

_____

_____

_____

4. Are you interested in a weekly small or large group Bible Study together?

_____

_____

_____

_____

_____

_____

5. Will there be specific passages or books of the Bible discussed?

_____

_____

_____

_____

_____

_____

6. Will someone be responsible for leading the discussion?

_____

_____

_____

_____

_____

_____

_____

7. If you choose to stay at home, will you take turns facilitating?

_____

_____

_____

_____

_____

It is suggested to answer the Discussion Questions before proceeding to Phase 7.

Plan for Time Outs

Date Nights and Vacations

"Trust in the Lord with all your heart, And lean not on your own understanding; In all your ways acknowledge Him, And He shall direct your paths"
(Proverbs 3:5-6).

When marriages face trials, it is often because of confusion, frustration, and lack of communication between one another and God. With busy schedules, children, family, and other outside obligations, it can be extremely difficult for couples to regroup and recharge with each other. With so much going on, marriages are often neglected. It is important for a husband and wife to take care of responsibilities and to provide for the family. It is also significant to trust in God to provide for your marriage and family.

During a basketball game, players get tired and eventually will have to sit out a portion of the game to recharge, regroup, and trust the process. If you ever noticed during time outs, players are connecting with one another, and when the game is back in motion, they are better than before.

God did not intend for a husband and wife to just become subject to the daily routine of raising children, chores, and working, but become life-long spiritual and sexual partners...yes, sexual intercourse.

Sex is a part of a marriage. *This does not speak to those marriages that are not physically capable to engage in sexual acts.* Many marriages suffer because of the lack of sexual intercourse. Married couples should not feel embarrassed to talk or engage in sexual activity with their husband or wife. God gave us the ability to have sexual pleasures with our husband or wife.

Nevertheless, because of sexual immorality, let each man have his own wife, and let each woman have her own husband. Let the husband render to his wife the affection due her, and likewise also the wife to her husband. The wife does not have authority over her own body, but the husband *does*. And likewise the husband does not have authority over his own body, but the wife *does*. Do not deprive one another except with consent for a time, that you may give yourselves to fasting and prayer; and come together again so that Satan does not tempt you because of your lack of self-control.

1 Corinthians 7:2-5

Some marriages will go through a phase where the sex stage is stalled, but for some, these stages will last months to even years. So, taking a time out to connect is crucial to your marriage. No kids, no work, just the two of you. It could be as simple as putting the kids to bed early one night so that you can enjoy each other's time or a standing appointment each week dedicated to the marriage. Nothing or no one should come before that appointment. Date nights and time away from everyday life will allow each marriage to regroup, recharge, and trust the process which will contribute to the overall well-being of the marriage.

Phase 7 Prayer

Heavenly Father, I ask You to bless our union, the union of which You have put together. So, God we glorify You and will lean on You to trust the plan You have for our lives and our marriage. We ask that we glorify You and continue to be a blessing to others. Help us to carve out time from our busy schedules to focus on You and each other more. We acknowledge that sometimes our lives and responsibilities get in the way of Your plan. In Jesus' name, amen.

Notes:

_____

_____

_____

_____

_____

_____

_____

_____

_____

_____

_____

_____

_____

_____

_____

_____

_____

_____

_____

_____

_____

_____

_____

_____

Phase 7

Discussion Questions, Thoughts, & Topics

Plan for Time Outs

Discussing ways to regroup and to rejuvenate.

1. From a scale to 1-10, how important are date nights, staycations or vacations?

_____

_____

_____

_____

_____

_____

_____

_____

2. How often are they needed?

_____

_____

_____

_____

_____

_____

_____

_____

Choosing the best time is also critical. It is suggested to incorporate date nights and vacations in your monthly budget. Also, create a schedule and remain committed.

It is suggested to answer the Discussion Questions before proceeding to Phase 8.

Practice

Correct Mistakes and Show Sportsmanship

"Let all bitterness, wrath, anger, clamor, and evil speaking be put away from you, with all malice. And be kind to one another, tenderhearted, forgiving one another, even as God in Christ forgave you"
(Ephesians 4:31-32).

Team players often make mistakes during the game. This could include missing shots, making a bad pass, or messing up a play. These kinds of mistakes are turnovers, giving the opposing team another opportunity to make points.

Life goes through changes. These challenges are caused by mistakes. Practice is key, so for every difficult moment, instead of making bad choices that can ultimately be detrimental to the marriage, practice your vows. If financial hardship arises, be encouraging and do not blame one another. If your husband or wife becomes ill, remain committed to them. Practice! Marriage needs communication. The more outside forces try to come between the marriage, the more the two of you should communicate.

Also, show grace and forgiveness. When a team member is out on the court missing shots, that does not mean that person should not be allowed to take another shot. Your partner will make mistakes and so will you, so lead by example.

Sometimes, seasons in your marriage may be so difficult that you wonder, *how will our marriage survive this?* You may also feel as though there have been so many mistakes that your marriage is irreconcilable. For this, I will say go back to the drawing board (through prayer) and find what made you fall in love. Yes, it can be difficult to be optimistic.

Our marriage has endured challenges. The only thing that has gotten us to a point of reconciliation is prayer and forgiveness. When you find your marriage going through hardships, pray before you find yourself making mistakes that will cost your marriage. Also, let go of anger and bitterness; it is easier to communicate with someone who is not angry.

Phase 8 Prayer

Heavenly Father, thank you for forgiving our sins and showing us favor and grace. We do not know where we would be without your love and kindness in our lives. Help us to show this same level of forgiveness to our spouses and to ourselves when hardship arises. Erase all anger and bitterness from our hearts. In Jesus' name, amen.

Notes:

_____

_____

_____

_____

_____

_____

_____

_____

_____

_____

_____

_____

_____

Phase 8

Discussion Questions, Thoughts, & Topics
Practice

Fixing mistakes are needed!

1. **Summative:** What were the methodologies discussed?

   _____

   _____

   _____

   _____

   _____

   _____

   _____

2. What are some foreseen problems? *Consider areas where mistakes are common and address those ideologies before they become problematic.*

   _____

   _____

   _____

   _____

   _____

   _____

   _____

3. How do you like to be confronted? *It is important to remain consistent in this practice.*

_____

_____

_____

_____

_____

_____

_____

4. Are there any gestures, comments, or personalities you dislike?

_____

_____

_____

_____

_____

_____

_____

It is suggested to answer the Discussion Questions before proceeding to Phase 9.

REV. GEORGE LASLEY III & STEPHANIE LASLEY

Celebrate Small Victories

Set Small Goals

*"For whatever is born of God overcomes the
world. And this is the victory that has
overcome the world our faith"*
(1 John 5:4).

There are many types of goals to set. The goals
should be tailored to your marriage. Every marriage has
unique challenges. The more emphasis that is placed
on goals, the faster couples can overcome challenges.
One of the greatest gifts to remember is that every day
is a victory, 1 John 5:4 echoes this sentiment. Because
of the believer's faith in God, they are assured that God
has overcame the world. God provides power to overcome and succeed in the endeavors that we set.

"But without faith *it is* impossible to please *Him*, for
he who comes to God must believe *that* He is, and that

He is a rewarder of those who diligently seek Him" (Hebrews 11:6). This verse reminds us of God's promises.

Any team that seeks to improve an endeavor must set small goals; this is usually done as a team. There are individual and team goals that are needed. Believe it or not, coaches set goals for themselves and each other. Setting goals should not be limited to one person or idea. Great teams set goals that express the importance of its end goal, which the next phase addresses. Any team that is not consistent in reaching its goals will find itself in the same predicament. Consistency is an important goal to achieve.

Celebrating small victories in a marriage is a *must*. Since there are so many things that each person must deal with, it is best to set aside time to enjoy each other's accomplishments. There is nothing better than praise from your spouse. Often, we can assume that the other person understands how we feel about them. They may know it; but it should also come from you first. Reassurance is an essential aspect of this phase.

As much as we want to get frustrations off our chest, we may unintentionally place our burden on one another. The more a couple takes time to spend with each other, the less their concerns of life will become. Complaining about life can be second nature. Couples gripe about work, personal life, kids, the house, the car, etc., so why not create a list of things that you and your marriage want to complete? It is advised to display the goals somewhere visible, providing a visual trajectory. My wife and I have our own set of goals, and we meet quarterly to discuss the process.

Effective communication will prevent the enemy from distracting you from being committed and appreciating God, self, one another, and goals. As one begins to celebrate small victories, there will be less room to complain and more time to concentrate on the marriage. Because of this shift in thinking, you will enjoy your marriage more. It is easy to get distracted by life, so setting small goals are important, but more significantly, celebrating those accomplishments are just as important.

Phase 9 Prayer

Lord help me and _____ to celebrate the victory of your Son Jesus the Christ. As we enjoy that together, allow us to always remain faithful to our vows and goals, in Jesus' name, amen.

Notes:

_____

_____

_____

_____

_____

_____

_____

_____

_____

_____

_____

_____

_____

_____

_____

_____

_____

_____

_____

_____

_____

Phase 9

Discussion Questions, Thoughts, & Topics

Celebrate Small Victories

The word celebration may take on different meanings.

1. Do you remember to celebrate daily with God?

_____

_____

_____

_____

2. What does celebrating small victories feel like for you?

_____

_____

_____

_____

_____

3. Are you willing to be consistent in setting a goal and celebrating accomplishments?

_____

_____

_____

_____

4. What challenges do you foresee?

_____

_____

_____

_____

It is suggested to answer the Discussion Questions before proceeding to Phase 10

Overcome Temptations

Outside Noise and Distractions

"No temptation has overtaken you except such as is common to man; but God is faithful, who will not allow you to be tempted beyond what you are able, but with the temptation will also make the way of escape, that you may be able to bear it"
(1 Corinthians 10:13).

Life is *difficult*, but most importantly, we can overcome. When the burdens of life weigh heavy, it is important to establish a strategy to get back up. We will go through trials and tribulations in life and it will be impossible to recover without the help of God.

Even great teams lose, but what is your comeback strategy and who will you rely on? Players usually turn to a coach for direction on how to respond to outside distractions. During a game, a player or even the team might receive a negative comment from its opponents or fans. Players are taught to ignore the distractions, but many times players may find themselves falling into taunting or playing overly aggressive. Then there are others who enjoy the noise. We all need to learn how to overcome difficulties in life by quieting the crowd with determination and dedication. In order to maintain consistent, minimizing outside distractions is a must, because a winning attitude is needed to be a champion. Distractions can come in many different forms. Someone in a marriage may be going through something personally. Teammates are responsible for helping, no one should be left to face disappointments alone.

The closer you and your spouse get, the more your marriage will be tested. Outside noise and distractions consist of miscommunications, arguments or a spouse taking up interest in something that takes too much of their time. The devil likes to stir up trouble between you and your spouse; *don't let that happen.* Leaning on God is the strategy to fight against distractions and outside noise. Prayer is what gives us power through the Holy Spirit and allows us to break down things that try to deter the union of marriage.

In 2 Corinthians 10:4-5, it states, "For the weapons of our warfare are not carnal but mighty in God for pulling down strongholds, casting down arguments and every high thing that exalts itself against the knowledge of God, bringing every thought into captivity to the obedience of Christ." The Bible teaches us that we are not fighting against flesh, but against Spirits so we cannot expect to fight off distractions with our own power; we must call and rely on the Holy Spirit through prayer. So, when you are faced with challenges, outside noise, and distractions in your marriage, seek God and plan a time to pray together.

Phase 10 Prayer

Holy Father, I pray for all marriages that are under attack by the enemy. I ask that husbands and wives everywhere would come together to pray and seek your guidance and protection against all hurt, harm or danger. God, we know it is You that can stand up against all things and we cannot make it without You. So, we ask for your protection and your blessing on our marriage. In Jesus' name, amen.

Notes:

_____

_____

_____

_____

_____

_____

_____

_____

_____

_____

_____

_____

_____

_____

_____

_____

_____

_____

_____

_____

_____

_____

_____

_____

Phase 10
Discussion Questions, Thoughts, & Topics
Overcome Temptations

Temptations will hinder a relationship, so it is essential to prevent flaws from becoming a barrier.

1. Discuss your limitations and pray to overcome them.

   _____

   _____

   _____

   _____

   _____

   _____

   _____

2. Seek to improve any area of weakness. *Explain your biggest flaw.*

   _____

   _____

   _____

   _____

   _____

   _____

   _____

3. Explain your personal strengths and weaknesses.

_____

_____

_____

_____

_____

_____

_____

_____

_____

_____

_____

_____

_____

_____

It is suggested to answer the Discussion Questions before proceeding to Phase 11.

Keep the End Goal in Mind

Obedience

"But seek first the kingdom of God and his righteousness, and all these things will be added to you"
(Matthew 6:33).

Basketball players face mental, emotional, and physical challenges during games and even after the game. My husband and I watched a game during the 2018-2019 NBA Finals, and we witnessed an injured player come into the game and eventually reinjure himself. At this time, the player was not thinking about his injury or what people thought about him playing while injured. He was thinking about winning the final championship: the end goal. His commitment and tenacity showed us how we should be in life and in our marriage. Our end goal should be to serve and glorify God because without the approval of God, nothing will matter. Our marriages will not work if we do not seek the kingdom of God and allow God to enter our marriage. God is the piece that will tie the husband and wife together through Holy matrimony.

Sometimes God gets pushed to the side in marriages and that is where trouble starts to arise. When committed to God, our marriage will reap all the benefits of love, patience, kindness, and forgiveness. Keeping the end goal in mind is needed. When we are no longer committed to God, we cannot be committed to our spouse. Keeping the end goal in mind will help us fight against all temptations, distractions, and outside noises that attack our marriages.

> Wives, submit to your own husbands, as to the Lord. For the husband is head of the wife, as also Christ is head of the church; and He is the Savior of the body. Therefore, just as the church is subject to Christ, so let the wives be to their own husbands in everything. Husbands love your wives, just as Christ also loved the church and gave Himself for her.
>
> Ephesians 5:22-25

Being committed will help us stay true to God's Word. It is essential to seek God first in all that we do and not rely on what society says marriage should look like. If we allow societal norms to take precedent over the Bible, then marriages will fail. Marriage is a declaration of commitment and God views marriage as a sacred relationship formed together to please Him. If God formed this relationship, then why subject it to societal pressures and norms of what marriage should look like? Humanity was not the one to join a man and a woman together, so it should not be up to anyone to tear a marriage a part. Keeping the end goal in mind is all about pleasing, serving, and being obedient to God.

Phase 11 Prayer

God, please allow us to stay obedient to Your Word and let our lives be acceptable and pleasing unto You. We thank You for our spouse and the sacred union of our marriage. We honor our commitment to You and each other and will seek You first in everything. Our marriage belongs to You and we submit to Your will for our marriage. In Jesus' name, amen.

Notes:

_____

_____

_____

_____

_____

_____

_____

_____

_____

_____

_____

_____

_____

_____

_____

_____

_____

_____

_____

_____

_____

_____

Phase 11

Discussion Questions, Thoughts, & Topics

Keep the End Goal in Mind

1. What is your marriage's end goals? *(What do you seek to accomplish?)*

_____

_____

_____

_____

_____

_____

_____

2. Discuss how to achieve your goals.

_____

_____

_____

_____

_____

_____

_____

_____

_____

_____

3. Create a list of goals for yourself and your marriage.
   This will help ensure that your goals are met.

   _____

   _____

   _____

   _____

   _____

   _____

   _____

   _____

   _____

It is suggested to answer the Discussion Questions before proceeding to Phase 12.

Pregame Preparation

Failing to Plan is Planning to Fail

"Prepare your outside work, Make it fit for yourself in the field; And afterward build your house"
(Proverbs 24:27).

Creating the pregame routine is something that most coaches rehearse with the team. Basketball fans know when a team has not practiced its pregame routine, the balls are flying around, the coaches look on from a distance, staring at the chaos.

Preparing for the future is important. Just like coaches who find themselves so invested in its team and players. Neglecting to address the pregame routine can cause in-game problems.

Proverbs 24:27 addresses the essentials of preparing for the future. The scripture makes it clear that preparing the work in the field comes before building the house. The work in the house is an extension from the work that has begun years before.

There are many marriages that fail because of the lack of preparation. In many cases, people are reluctant to tell their fiancé their desires to prevent becoming a turn-off. Those wants will soon surface in other phases in life.

There are several things to discuss before getting married. Those who are married can still learn, but those who are not married have an advantage. Before addressing some of the ideologies that are worth noting, it is important to reflect the sentiment in Phase 4. Both persons should respect the opinions of the other person. Allow the other person to express his or her issues. Reaching a compromise is the goal.

Having children is one of the most prominent aspects that can affect a marriage. In many cases, there is one person who desires to have kids more than the other. Express the number of kids, the preferred gender, the child's name, along with where to live. Anyone would hate to get married and feel that his or her desires were not met because of the other person. As noted, this can cause a lot of resentment that could influence the game, which in this case is the future.

It is without question that *preparing the field is not an option; it is a priority.*

Phase Activity: Create a list of your greatest desires. You and your spouse should do this at the same time. Each person should make a list of five things and compare each other's responses together to see which viewpoints overlap. It is vital to understand which outlooks are consistent, and it is just as important to see the ideas that you do not have in common. Please discuss those viewpoints before going to the next phase.

Phase 12 Prayer

God help me understand my spouse's needs so that he/she feels comfortable being himself or herself. Father, please allow my spouse to be accepting of the person that You wish for me to become. In Jesus' name we pray, amen.

Notes:

_____

_____

_____

_____

_____

_____

_____

_____

_____

_____

_____

_____

_____

_____

_____

_____

_____

_____

_____

_____

_____

_____

_____

Phase 12
Discussion Questions, Thoughts, & Topics
Pregame Preparation

Marriage planning is important but don't get over-whelmed. Proper marital counseling is encouraged. It is always advised not to spend more than twenty percent of your household income on the wedding ceremony.

1. On a scale from 1-10, how important is the wedding ceremony, reception, and honeymoon?

_____

_____

_____

_____

_____

2. On a scale from 1-10, how important is it to be married to the person that God has given you? *The answer to number 1 should not be higher or equal to the answer of question 2.*

_____

_____

_____

_____

_____

3. Have you considered how you will remain happy after your big day?

_____

_____

_____

_____

_____

_____

_____

4. *Other things to think of: Wedding budget, officiant, number of invitations, wedding date and time, wedding colors, photographer, reception, and DJ.*

_____

_____

_____

_____

_____

_____

_____

It is suggested to answer the Discussion Questions before proceeding to Phase 13.

The Game Begins

Remain One

*"So then, they are no longer two but one flesh.
Therefore what God has joined together,
let no man separate"
(Matthew 19:6).*

Practice is critical; there are many who disagree, because they may like to rely upon pure talent. However, pure talent alone will not help with team chemistry or team bonding. There have been many star players that were just great individual players, with many individual stats. Many players are only judged on their accomplishments, but when considering the Hall of Fame, most players must not only possess the accolades necessary, but must possess a championship. Many fans are unaware of the sacrifices that were made to become great. Many Hall of Fame speeches echo words that express the importance of team chemistry and overcoming obstacles.

Before getting to the Hall of Fame, remaining one with those who have invested in you is needed. To ensure greatness, when the game begins, it is vital to make sure that aspects addressed in practice are incorporated on and off the floor. When team chemistry is abandoned, the only hope is to achieve individual statistics.

The phrase "the game begins" can suggest to a marriage that when all the dating, conversations, marital planning, and the marriage ceremony is over, the marriage will officially begin. It becomes important to remember the reasons that brought you two together. Looking at the other eleven phases is necessary, considering that sometimes situations will occur in life that were not planned. Remaining consistent with the vows is difficult if the groundwork in the relationship has not been established. The groundwork refers to the plans that need to be incorporated to ensure a successful marriage.

Be willing to spiritually fight for your marriage, because in keeping with the analogy of "the game begins", it is important to understand that there are oppositions. Often, those who dislike you or those who hate to see you two together are given too much attention. The most significant opponent on the court is the couple itself. The devil, who is the opposition, cannot defeat those who confessed their faith and marriage to God. It might not be ideal to say out loud "the game begins" when situations arise, but saying it within reminds each person that they have a position to play at the beginning of what will become, based on the foundation of the relationship and the willingness to assess the team for more effectiveness.

A basketball game has a start time and an end time. The end goal should always be in mind, because strategies are enforced to ensure a victory. Playing only for fun is for those who want to enter marriage for selfish reasons.

When shots are not falling, it is easy to elect not to shoot again, until your last shot wins the game. It is easy to give up because things appear not to be working out; note that it only takes one shot to win. This comes after hard work and determination. Getting back in the game is a team effort, and everybody has to be onboard. If not, this leaves only one person wanting the marriage to work.

Why practice marriage if the end goal was never to become one flesh mentally and spiritually? Matthew 19:6 exposes a very true element in a marriage that is often recited and sometimes never executed. In marriage, God must be the center focus, because without Him, the game will never begin. It would be two flesh acting like one. That might be helpful for some, but that was never God's intention. God wants those who

He puts together to become one flesh in love through the grace of Jesus the Christ.

Being nervous about getting married is not an indication that you are not ready for marriage because it shows your desire to make the marriage work. As the crowds of people at your wedding disappear, and the paper that the vows were written on are folded up, know the game has begun.

Phase 13 Prayer:

Lord help us to remain faithful to you as we seek to become one and decrease our pride that we may love each other like you loved the Church. In Jesus' name, amen.

Notes:

_____

_____

_____

_____

_____

_____

_____

_____

_____

_____

Phase 13
Discussion Questions, Thoughts, & Topics
The Game Begins

1. Once your marriage begins, are you willing to change if needed?

   _____

   _____

   _____

   _____

   _____

2. Are you willing to be patient with life and your spouse?

   _____

   _____

   _____

   _____

   _____

3. Will you stay committed to God if difficulties arise?

   _____

   _____

   _____

   _____

4. Are you committed to function in your role?

_____

_____

_____

_____

_____

_____

_____

5. How consistent are you in your plans?

_____

_____

_____

_____

_____

It is suggested to answer the Discussion Questions before proceeding to Phase 14.

The Playoffs

Overcome Pressure

*"We are hard-pressed on every side, yet not crushed;
we are perplexed, but not in despair; persecuted, but
not forsaken; struck down, but not destroyed"*
(*2 Corinthians 4:8-9*).

Phase 14 is a summative phase because it specifies the importance of adjusting to challenges, as noted in Phase 1, a marriage is constantly evolving. The playoffs are drastically different from regular season games, because the opposition's purpose to win intensifies. It is important to adjust to different forms of pressure, which explains why many teams are unprepared for the playoffs. Also, weaknesses are exposed in the team's identity and cultural values are exposed when regular routines are stopped.

Those who are married or looking to get married are advised to really consider this phase as one of the most essential since it is a summative aspect. If one of the phases get overlooked or abandoned, serious problems can occur. Minor situations can begin to hurt if a couple is not willing to play off each other strengths and weaknesses. Phase 4 and Phase 5 address the purpose of communicating, because without it, outside noise in Phase 11 can begin to erode the marriage's chemistry.

The passage of 2 Corinthians 4:8-9 explains how to perceive obstacles with an open mindset because chaos can build character. The scripture confronts the different scenarios that exist. There will be times in a marriage when a husband and a wife will feel hard pressed, perplexed, persecuted, and struck down, but the Apostle Paul provides a Christian hope. If one trusts the process of God by remaining faithful and trusting that God will see you through individually and collectively, those who call themselves Christians will not be crushed, in despair, forsaken, and or destroyed.

It is inevitable that problems will occur in any relationship, but the enemy's focus is to destroy a union between two people that are bound by the Spirit of the Lord. Satan marvels at the hope of causing enough frustration to cause at least one person to give up.

A marriage can become problematic, when a person does not understand his or her role or impact. For those who are facing difficulties within a marriage with a person who is not willing to grow spiritually, pray for your spouse as much as you want someone to pray for you. Trust that God will help your significant other see their weaknesses, just like God did for us. Remember the purpose of your marriage. Spiritual counseling is overlooked by many people, maybe because many people's definition is distorted. Spiritual counseling must come from God, helping you choose the person to talk to and what to read that will aid you in the direction that God has chosen for you.

God wants us to trust Him more than you trust your mate. God causes all of us to love and forgive. Love can restore the challenges that arise, and when the team chemistry or love gets too thin, go to the person that will guide and direct you to the joy that God gives.

Phase 14 Prayer

God, when challenges come our way, help us to direct own attention to you. Aid us in saying and doing what pleases you. Allow your Holy Spirit to be the biggest presence in our life and situation. We rebuke the attacks of Satan and we decree and declare that God will give us enough endurance to endure the hardships of the playoffs because we know the victory that awaits us in glory. In Jesus' name, amen.

Notes:

_____

_____

_____

_____

_____

_____

_____

_____

_____

_____

_____

_____

_____

_____

_____

_____

_____

_____

_____

_____

_____

_____

_____

_____

_____

Phase 14

Discussion Questions, Thoughts, & Topics

The Playoffs

Some tenured relationships may lack enthusiasm.

1. Are you committed to loving one another and his or her indifferences?

   _____

   _____

   _____

   _____

   _____

2. How will you make sure that your excitement will persist over time?

   _____

   _____

   _____

   _____

   _____

   _____

It is suggested to answer the Discussion Questions before proceeding to Phase 15.

REV. GEORGE LASLEY III & STEPHANIE LASLEY

The Finals

The Next Level

"If you faint in the day of adversity,
Your strength is small"
(Proverbs 24:10).

I can recall going to college for the first time, and stuffing the car with all of the little belongings that I had. One of my neighbors was standing on his porch and told me, "If it was easy, everybody would have done it." The philosophy still applies to those who are getting married or those want to stay married. Marriage is difficult for the reasons previously mentioned. Each marriage is unique with its own purpose.

However, God reassures us through the words of King Solomon not to faint. The last phase addresses future challenges. Phase 15 is a follow-up of Phase 14, because the finals are just like the playoffs, except the whole world is watching two teams, which enhances the intensity because it's the next level from your prior circumstance.

Nothing stays the same, a marriage needs to evolve over time with the help of the Lord. Its identity needs to be solidified and specified. Resources are needed to get to the final stages in a marriage. Even though Phase 15 mentions certain perspectives from Phase 14, please consider reading Phase 15 in hopes of understanding the entirety of *The Marriage Playbook*. In order to endure the adversity that Proverbs 24:10 records, relying upon God's strength is the only way to remain married.

I have sent flowers to my wife, and one of her coworkers mentioned that she has been married for a long period of time, and this coworker said her husband used to do similar things. She begins to tell my wife that kind of gesture will fade over time. Unfortunately, this comment has become a norm; some couples are staying together just to celebrate one day of the year with each other, and then go back to sleeping in different rooms, barely communicating around the house.

This intent of getting married for the sake of getting married will appear in your mannerisms. Consider getting married for all the reasons according to the Bible. Many marriages are unable to move to the next level, because someone either missed Phase 1 or missed many of the other pivotal aspects that direct the reader back to God.

Lastly, for those who aspire to be great again, while the others around you do not, your job is to encourage and motivate, and begin at Phase 1. If not, the team's potential will rest on your shoulders to take the love, the desire to be romantic, the effort to forgive, and the effort to trust to the next level.

Phase 15 Prayer

God please help our marriage take the necessary steps to achieve the goals that You have for us. Help us help each other. If there is anything we lack, allow us to see the area(s) and work on it so we can move to the next phase in our life. We know that we cannot do anything without you. Please grant us many more joyous days with each other and give us enough strength to endure all that we will face in the future. Give us the ability to be an inspiration to others. In Jesus' name, amen.

Notes:

_____

_____

_____

_____

_____

_____

_____

_____

_____

_____

_____

_____

_____

_____

_____

_____

_____

_____

_____

_____

_____

_____

_____

_____

Phase 15
Discussion Questions, Thoughts, & Topics
The Finals

The word "Finals" signify completion. It should be clarified that the word is the "end goal" addressed in Phase 10.

1. What does this phase mean to you?

   _____

   _____

   _____

   _____

   _____

   _____

2. How can you share the things that you learned in your marriage with others?

   _____

   _____

   _____

   _____

   _____

   _____

   _____

3. Remember to keep praying, because the enemy hates godly marriages.

_____

_____

_____

_____

_____

_____

_____

_____

Epilogue

Here is an essential aspect that was mentioned as a reminder: Put God first! Romans 8:28 states, "And we know that all things work together for good to those who love God, to those who are the called according to His purpose."

Afterword

A marriage counseling session inspired the creation of *The Marriage Playbook*. The original outline can be found in the appendix.

The Marriage Playbook was constructed to emphasize the structure of marriage. It is written for anyone. Couples are recommended to read each chapter independently before reading it together.

This book is a tool to provide marital advice by using basketball analogies. The conceptualizations are written from a coaches' perspective. The coaches have created each aspect as a phase in practice. The reader is asked to devote himself or herself to the fifteen-phase practice. The book will strengthen your marriage and give you a new perspective on life.

Appendix

A Playbook for Marriage

You Two are on the Same Team

Head Coach: Secure

Superstar Player: Beautiful

The Plays to Win!

Tip-off

Ask God and let go!

Forgive the past

Forgive each other

Half Time

Go back to the basics

Trust and communicate

Let each other play their role(s)

Let each other back into your hearts

Love, Love, and Love!
Repeat

Blessings,
Rev. George and Stephanie Lasley III

CPSIA information can be obtained
at www.ICGtesting.com
Printed in the USA
FSHW021510050320
67769FS